Love

the key to it all

Love
the key to it all

NICK FAWCETT

**kevin
mayhew**

First published in 2002 by
KEVIN MAYHEW LTD
Buxhall, Stowmarket, Suffolk IP14 3BW
Email: info@kevinmayhewltd.com

9 8 7 6 5 4 3 2 1 0

ISBN 1 84003 920 5
Catalogue No 1500512

Cover design by Angela Selfe
Edited by Katherine Laidler
Typesetting by Louise Selfe
Printed and bound in Great Britain

Contents

Introduction 7

Leader's notes 9

Prayer 11

First week 13
  God is love

Second week 23
  Love God

Third week 33
  Love one another

Fourth week 46
  Love your enemies

Fifth week 56
  Love your neighbour

Sixth week 68
  Love yourself

Appendix 1 78
  Activities

Appendix 2 84
  Answers

To Olwen Matthias, in memory of Eric,
with thanks for everything you both did for us
in so many ways

Acknowledgements

Bible quotations are taken from the New Revised Standard Version of the Bible, copyright © 1989 by the Division of Christian Education of the National Council of the Churches of Christ in the USA. Used by permission. All rights reserved.

Introduction

The moment was the sort we all dread. I'd arrived home, reached in my pocket . . . and then reached again, a feeling of dismay stealing over me. It couldn't be true, surely – but it was: I'd left home that morning without taking the key and thus found myself standing outside my front door wondering what to do next. I could look in through the letterbox, peer in through the window, see my keys maddeningly close on the sideboard, but, short of forcing the lock or smashing a window, I couldn't get in. Thankfully, my wife had a set of keys too, but it was to be a long wait until she came home.

For many, the Christian faith seems like a closed door. They may occasionally look inside a church door, catch a snippet of *Songs of Praise* on television, or hear something about the gospel, but it doesn't make sense, coming across as superstition, fantasy or sheer gobbledegook. Some are more sympathetic, interested in taking things further but troubled by doubts and questions that they struggle in vain to resolve. Others have committed themselves to Christ, yet are not quite sure where they stand, what they believe, or what they *need* to believe. On one level, this is not surprising, for in faith we are dealing with mystery, with the God whose ways and thoughts are different to our own. Yet alongside the mystery there is also simplicity, for the gospel revolves around one axis – the centrality of love. No other word more eloquently expresses the nature of God. No other term more completely sums up the response he requires from us. Certainly we need to explore what that means and how it is worked out in practice, yet love is the key to faith, the answer that unlocks the door.

This book reflects that conviction. It begins by exploring a statement of faith at its simplest – 'God is love' – and then moves on to our response, both in terms of loving God and loving others. We see how this involves loving our enemies, our neighbours and ourselves, recognising that each of those is part of loving God, which itself springs from his love for us. In other words, at every level love is central: the most important commandment of all.

Much of faith is complex; there's no getting away from it, and there will always be aspects we struggle to understand. Don't let that obscure, though, the simple message at its heart, the importance of love as the key to it all.

Nick Fawcett

Leader's notes

I suggest using the material in this book as follows:

- Each session begins with a traditional prayer, followed by a short paragraph introducing the overall theme. It is worth reading this aloud, to set the scene for the session.

- After this I have included 'Activity' sessions, designed to break the ice and to encourage informal reflection on the theme of the study. Allow ten minutes or so for these, but do not allow them to dominate the session.

- Next comes a Bible passage (my own paraphrase unless otherwise stated). This should be read aloud and then time given for group members to quietly ponder its meaning.

- Ideally, group members need to have read the 'Comment' section before the meeting, in which case you will need to have circulated booklets in advance of the first session. Alternatively, extend the period of quiet after the reading so that participants can read this section at their own pace.

- The 'Summary' section highlights the key points of the Comment. The leader should read this aloud before inviting people's thoughts on the subject so far.

- Allow discussion to develop and introduce as appropriate the questions provided in the Discussion section. It may be appropriate at this point to bring in the passage suggested for further reading, though you may prefer to leave this, as I have done, to round off the theme nearer the end.

- Pause for prayer, using the prayer provided, a prayer of your own, or a time of quiet/open prayer.

- After allowing ample time for discussion, read the meditation to draw people's thoughts together. The meditation in week 2 was written specially for this book; the others are taken from my earlier publications *No Ordinary Man*, *Are You Listening?* and *To Put It Another Way*.

- Briefly, outline the suggestions for action. Invite any further ideas from among the group. From the second week onwards, you might also give people the opportunity to share how they got on with the suggestions from the previous week.
- Finally, end the meeting in prayer, using either the prayer provided or your own.

Prayer

Gracious God,
  we praise you for the great gift of love –
  love that we are able to share with those around us,
  that gives us a sense of self-worth and belonging
  and that enriches our lives in so many ways.
You have opened your heart to all –
  help us to do the same.

We praise you that you are above all else a God of love,
  not of judgement, anger or vengeance,
  but of a love that goes on reaching out to us day after day,
  constant, total, inexhaustible,
  flowing out to us like a never-ending stream.
You have opened your heart to all –
  help us to do the same.

Though we fail you again and again,
  caring more about ourselves than you or others,
  still you go on loving us,
  fiercely and wholeheartedly.
You have opened your heart to all –
  help us to do the same.

Though we turn away from you,
  wilfully rejecting your guidance
  and repeatedly betraying your trust,
  still you long to take us back,
  to restore a living, loving relationship.
You have opened your heart to all –
  help us to do the same.

Speak to us through all you have done,
  and so deepen our love for you and for others.

Help us to be faithful and true in all our relationships,
   and most especially in our relationship with you.
You have opened your heart to all –
   help us to do the same.

Gracious God,
   help us so to know you that your love flows through us,
   reaching upwards in worship,
   inwards in fellowship
   and outwards in service
   to the glory of your name.
You have opened your heart to all –
   help us to do the same.

In the name of Christ.
Amen.

First week

God is love

Opening prayer

O God,
 fountain of love,
 pour your love into our souls,
 that we may love those whom you love
 with the love you give us,
 and think and speak of them tenderly,
 meekly,
 lovingly;
 and so, loving our brothers and sisters for your sake,
 may we grow in your love,
 and dwelling in love dwell in you,
 for Jesus Christ's sake.
Amen.

E. B. Pusey (1800; updated)

Introduction

Some time ago, I decided it was time to invest in a new word-processing package so I bought a copy of Microsoft 98. It has not only proven an invaluable tool but also a useful, if at times sobering, critic of my writing. Not only has it picked up several habitual spelling mistakes and errors in grammar but it has also highlighted issues of style. On more occasions than I care to admit, I complete what I deem to be a well-written sentence, only to find a wiggly green line underneath indicating that something is wrong, and when I click on the mouse to reveal the problem, the comment is invariably the same: 'Wordiness (consider revising)'! Initially, I ignored that advice, telling myself it was an arbitrary judgement, a matter of opinion, but after a few years now of editing and proofreading, I have come to pay it much greater heed.

Probably most of us use more words than are strictly necessary. I well remember producing my first article for the Toc H magazine, *Point Three*, confidently submitting it to the magazine's new editor. A few days later, it was back on my desk, with a list of suggested deletions. It came as something of a shock, especially when I realised that, despite its savage pruning, the final article (less than half the size of the original) had lost none of its meaning.

With God, in particular, we can and often do use many words where one will suffice. As we will see in this first session, several attempts have been made across the years to define God or express the essentials of faith, innumerable words used in the process. Billions more have been added in theological and devotional writings, as authors attempt to bring understanding, inspiration and encouragement, or simply to express their faith. There is nothing wrong with that, of course – quite the opposite – but we must not lose sight of the underlying simplicity of the gospel and of the nature of God himself. For all the complexities of faith and the controversial issues of theology, one word provides the key to it all: love. Admittedly, this begs the question 'What do we mean by love?' – how else can I justify adding another book to the millions already published! – but in talking about God or anything to do with faith we must constantly come back to this reference point, the yardstick of love against which all else is measured.

Activity

Hymns of love (see page 78).

Reading: 1 John 4:8-10, 16b

Whoever does not love knows nothing of God, for God is love. God demonstrated his love like this – he sent his only Son into the world in order that we might live through him. In this is love, not that we loved God but that he loved us and sent his Son to be the expiation for our sins. God is love, and all who dwell in love dwell in God, and God dwells in them.

Comment

How would you define God? What word or words would you use to encapsulate who and what he is? On one level, that is a ridiculous question, for no words are adequate to describe what is ultimately before all, in all and beyond all. Whatever we say, there is always more to be said, words barely able to skim the surface. If defining God, though, seems hard, how would you like to define the Christian faith? Surely that is harder still. Yet, in the early days of the Church, and in some Christian circles today, many have felt the need to summarise the essentials of the gospel, whether through creeds passed down across the centuries or through statements of faith that adherents are expected to subscribe to. 'I believe in God, the Father Almighty, creator of heaven and earth' – so begins the Apostles' Creed. Or, as the Nicene Creed puts it, 'We believe in one God, the Father, the Almighty, maker of heaven and earth, of all that is, seen and unseen'. So I could go on, various formulations put together in an attempt to express the fundamentals of the Christian faith. Surprisingly, however, not one creed, as far as I know, mentions a word that is probably the most important of all: the word 'love'. Personally, were I asked to summarise the gospel, I would opt for the simple statement 'I believe that God is love', and I would not be alone, for this, essentially, is the understanding of God that runs throughout our reading, and indeed throughout the whole first epistle of John.

You can turn wherever you like in the Scriptures and it is the same story. Take first the Old Testament. 'O give thanks to the Lord, for he is good; his steadfast love endures for ever!' says the writer of Psalm 118 (v. 1, *NRSV*). 'He brought me to the banqueting house,' declares the Song of Solomon, likening the love of God to that between husband and wife (2:4, *NRSV*), 'and his intention towards me was love.' 'When Israel was a child,' declares God in the book of Hosea, comparing his feelings to the devotion of a loving parent (11:1a, 3a, 4a, *NRSV*), 'I loved him . . . It was I who taught Ephraim to walk, I took them up in my arms . . . I led them with cords of human kindness, with bands of love.' Or, as the prophet Jeremiah so beautifully puts it, 'I have loved you with a never-ending love; therefore I have remained faithful to you always' (Jeremiah 31:3b).

Turning to the New Testament, it is the same message. 'God proves his love for us', writes Paul, 'in that while we still were sinners Christ died for us' (Romans 5:8, *NRSV*). Or, as the first Epistle of John puts it, 'In this is love, not that we loved God but that he loved us and sent his Son to be the expiation for our sins' (1 John 4:10). Perhaps most unforgettable of all, we have the testimony of John 3:16: 'For God so loved the world that he gave his only Son, so that everyone who believes in him may not perish but may have eternal life' (John 3:16). These are just a small sample of the innumerable verses in the Bible that remind us of the God whose nature is always to show love.

Have we understood what that means? Have we allowed that truth to shape our faith and permeate our lives? Or do we still see God, in practice, as forbidding and unapproachable, sternly scrutinising our every action and looking for an opportunity to punish should we put a foot wrong? Although intellectually we may accept God loves us, it is a different matter to wholeheartedly believe that. We struggle to take on board the idea of a love that gives and goes on giving, that recognises our faults yet is undeterred by them, that is met by faithlessness and rejection yet goes on reaching out. Here is a love different from anything we find elsewhere – constant, dependable, inexhaustible – yet this is the God we serve. He longs to bless, not punish; to give, rather than take away; to build up instead of pull down, to forgive rather than condemn. No, we don't deserve such love, for we abuse, betray and deny it each day, but that's what makes God's love so special, for, despite the feebleness of our response, it goes on cleansing, renewing, restoring, forgiving – a love that will never let us go.

For some, defining God as love is far too loose, dangerously vague, woolly and insipid. Instead they want prescriptive and proscriptive guidelines: a faith that categorically states what we should and shouldn't do, and that unequivocally sets out the penalties for stepping over the mark. 'Believe this, accept that', we are told, as Christianity is reduced to rules and regulations covering every moral decision and ethical dilemma. Personally, I find the assumption that there is a clear right and wrong in every situation deeply disturbing, for life is all too rarely black and white. Didn't Jesus himself repeatedly challenge socially accepted norms, forgiving those whom others considered beyond the pale, accepting the unacceptable? Certainly he didn't always condone, but neither did he condemn. Clear-cut certainties may be appealing, in that we know precisely where we stand, but they have little to do with the way of love.

Others raise more fundamental questions. How can we speak of a God of love, they want to know, in a world so full of pain, suffering, sorrow and evil? Few of us can have failed to feel the force of such questions at some time in our life, confronted perhaps by the premature death of a loved one, or seeing a friend suffer, or simply witnessing the tragedies and atrocities that unfold week by week on the world stage. There are no easy answers here. All that we can do is point to the cross, and affirm that in the pain, suffering, sorrow and evil we see there, God was supremely at work. We cannot fully explain it, yet we hold on to the conviction that through identifying himself with our human experience God has paved the way for his ultimate triumph over everything that separates us from his love.

There is one more point yet that we need to consider, and that is who this love is for. As the well-loved words of John 3:16 remind us, 'God so loved *the world* that he gave his only Son.' Have we wrestled with the implications of what that means? God's love is open-ended, nowhere and no one off limits. It is for Jew and Gentile, male and female, black and white; for Buddhist, Hindu, Muslim, atheist, Christian, Free Church, High Church, Low Church, House Church, no church – in short, for anyone and everyone. God's concern reaches out to all, irrespective of their colour, culture or creed. Again, does that make a difference to the way we live? Does it extend the scope of our concern and the breadth of our vision? Is it reflected in our prayers and worship, our service and our lifestyle? As Christians, are our lives turned inwards or outwards?

To say 'God is love' is not just a statement about him but also about us, for love calls for a response. Unless we choose to reject it, love must be reciprocated, given as well as received if it is to grow and flourish. What does that mean in terms of God? How does he want us to respond to him? It is to this that we shall turn in the rest of this book.

Summary

- Various creeds and statements of belief have attempted to define the essentials of faith, including the nature of God, yet one statement, while simpler than all, says more than any: 'God is love.'
- That truth can be seen in both the Old and New Testaments, receiving its fullest expression in the latter. Whatever we say about God needs to be understood in the context of love. Lose sight of that and our picture of him will be skewed.
- God's love is supremely expressed in Christ, whose coming, living, dying and rising among us eloquently testifies to his total commitment to humankind.
- Have we understood that God is love, or do we think of him as angry, vengeful, remote and unapproachable? It is one thing to accept something with our head, another to believe it in our heart. Is ours, above all, a loving relationship with God?
- Though we don't deserve God's love, and though we repeatedly

deny and betray it through our actions, it continues reaching out to us, refusing to let us go.

- Some find the statement 'God is love' too vague, preferring a faith of moral and ethical certainties. This may give a sense of security, but it is not the way of love.
- Others find it hard to reconcile a God of love with the harsh realities of life. There are no easy answers to such questions, but we believe that in the sorrow and suffering of the Cross, God supremely demonstrated his love, paving the way to the ultimate victory of his purpose.
- His love, however, does not stop with the Church or ourselves. It is for all, extending to the ends of the earth and crossing all human boundaries.
- As well as bringing assurance, God's love also brings challenge, for to know and serve him means to love in turn. His love must spill over into our lives and flow from us to others.

Discussion

- What word first springs to your mind in describing God? What labels do we sometimes attach to him? How do we reconcile these with him being a God of love?
- In what ways is God's love like our own? In what ways is it different?
- Do we sometimes underestimate or limit the love of God? In what ways, and why?

Prayer

Lord God,
    we use so many words to describe you,
    so many terms to sum up who and what you are,

yet we know that all fall short, except one:
the word 'love'.
We praise you that this sums up your whole nature,
purpose and being,
no other word able to express the immensity of your goodness,
the extent of your grace,
the awesomeness of your purpose
and the intensity of your devotion.
Forgive us for losing sight of this truth,
for forgetting that however much we may fail you,
you will not fail us.
Teach us to open our lives to you now,
and so may we love both you and others
with the same commitment you show to us.
In the name of Christ we ask it.
Amen.

Meditation of John

Sentimental rubbish, that's what some will accuse me of,
another airy-fairy spiel about love,
whatever that's supposed to mean.
And I can see their point,
for we do use the word loosely,
enough sometimes to cover a multitude of sins,
yet when it comes to God, no other word will do,
for God *is* love!
It's as simple,
as straightforward,
as uncomplicated as that –
the one description that says it all,
and if you lose that one simple truth, you lose everything.
Not that you'd think it, mind you, to hear some people talk,
the picture they paint altogether different.
A God of wrath, they say,

justice, righteousness, punishment,
  sometimes jealous,
  often forbidding,
  remote, holy, set apart.
He *is* those, of course –
  or at least he can be when necessary –
  but never out of malice,
  only in love.
He longs to bless, not punish,
  to give, rather than take away;
  his nature always to have mercy,
  to show kindness,
  to fill our lives with good things.
If you see him otherwise,
  as some vengeful ogre intent on destroying you,
  then you don't know him,
  for I tell you, God *is* love –
  all the law,
  all the commandments,
  all our faith summed up in that small but wonderful word.
And though I can't put it into words,
  you'll understand what I mean if you *do* know him,
  for his love will flow in you, through you and from you,
  touching every part of your life.
No, we don't deserve such goodness,
  not for a moment,
  for we'll continue to fail him,
  our love always imperfect,
  but isn't that just the point,
  the thing which makes love so special?
It *does* cover a multitude of sins! –
  cleansing,
  renewing,
  restoring,
  forgiving –
  refusing to let go, come what may.

That's the God we serve,
   the sort of being he is –
   and if that isn't love, I don't know what is!

Further reading: Psalm 89:1-2a

I will sing unceasingly of your unfailing love, O Lord; I will declare your faithfulness to all generations. Your constant love is unchanged from the beginning of time, and your faithfulness is as permanent as the heavens.

Suggestions for action

Reflect on what you believe in the light of the statement 'God is love'. Ask yourself how far that truth is reflected in your faith and how far it shapes your life.

Closing prayer

Gracious God,
   we go on our way
   knowing that your love is all in all,
   now and for evermore.
Amen.

Second week

Love God

Opening prayer

O God,
> who has commanded all people to love you,
> and has drawn them to yourself by your mercy and goodness,
> fill our hearts with love of you.

We are weak and sinful,
> and cannot love you enough without your help.

All our desire is to give you the service of our loving hearts
> all the days of our life,
> and to love you throughout the ages of eternity,
> through Jesus Christ our Lord.

Amen.

Taken and updated from The Narrow Way *(1869)*

Introduction

It seemed to be another typical England batting performance: after a decent start, wickets were tumbling with monotonous regularity, but then, just when the situation appeared hopeless, things began to change. Instead of flailing wildly at every delivery, as earlier batsmen had done, the final pair were knuckling down to the job, talking earnestly between overs, discussing tactics, admonishing and encouraging each other as appropriate, determined to stick together for as long as possible. For the first time in the game, here were two players committed to building a lasting partnership, ready to show the patience, discipline and determination needed to make things work. The result was astonishing: a record partnership that saved the game.

Obviously, partnerships in the context of human relationships are very different, yet the underlying principle still applies. Despite the way we often romanticise love, it too is something that must be nurtured and cultivated. Many a relationship has endured rocky moments, even perhaps times of separation, the overcoming of which has required resolve from both parties to make it work. Do we exercise the same resolve in our relationship with God? His commitment to us is total, unreserved, but what about our commitment to him? Do we fall into the trap, sometimes, of leaving him to make the running, complacently thinking that no matter what we do the relationship cannot be broken? If so, we are making a big mistake, for though *he* will stay true, *we* can gradually drift away from him until we become hopelessly estranged. Our relationship with God is not one we can approach casually. He calls us to love him with all we have – body, mind and soul. Are we willing to do that? Are we committed to giving our all to help build a living and lasting relationship?

Activity

Myths, legends, gods and goddesses quiz (see page 79)

Reading: Deuteronomy 6:5; 10:12-13

You shall love the Lord your God with all your heart, and with all your soul, and with all your strength. What then, O Israel, does the Lord your God ask of you? Simply to fear the Lord your God, to follow in all his ways, to love and serve him with all your heart and soul, and, for your own good, to observe the Lord's commandments and decrees that I am giving you today.

Comment

What does it mean to love someone? That's a big question, isn't it? – one that could keep us occupied for years, let alone a short session such as this. So let me rephrase the question. What would you make of someone who claimed to love you and made great displays of affection, yet ignored your wishes, living instead in a way that made you unhappy? Would you call that love? I doubt it. What about if that person spoke of love, and attempted to show it, yet failed to display any real feeling, any genuine sign of heartfelt emotion? Would this be love? Again, the answer is no. Love involves the whole person, body, mind and spirit. It is not mechanical or learned by rote, but is characterised by an impulsive, spontaneous quality. Equally, it entails more than romantic sentiment. When we love someone, we think of what he or she might want rather than simply pursuing our own ends. It involves a giving of self, in the sense of opening up, being honest about who and what we are, and sharing every aspect of life together. Finally, it involves commitment, a determination to work at a relationship when it starts to founder rather than give up at the first hint of difficulty.

Such love is a rare thing, even in human relationships, but how many of us get close to it in our relationship with God? For all our talk of loving him – of worship, adoration and devotion – how many of us can truly claim to love God, or even to have considered what doing so might mean? Yet this challenge is and has always been central to our faith. 'You shall love the Lord your God with all your heart, and with all your soul, and with all your strength' says the book of Deuteronomy (6:5), and the importance attached to that is spelt out in the verses that follow: 'Keep these words that I am commanding you today in your heart. Recite them to your children and talk about them when you are at home and when you are away, when you lie down and when you rise. Bind them as a sign on your hand, fix them as an emblem on your forehead, and write them on the doorposts of your house and on your gates' (Deuteronomy 6:6-9, *NRSV*). The importance of loving God is placed firmly here at the heart of life – the source from which everything else flows. It's true that the book of Deuteronomy – like Exodus, Leviticus and Numbers before it – goes on to outline innumerable laws, rituals and regulations that can seem arid and legalistic, but the key to them all, and the goal they are intended to serve, lies in our daily relationship with God. Unless we love God, all else will founder.

So what does it mean to love God in practice? Three passages, for me, bring out the essentials, one from the New Testament and two from the Old. The first is the story of Mary, sister of Martha, anointing the feet of Jesus with costly perfume and then wiping it away with her hair (John 12:1-6). According to Judas Iscariot, it was an act of senseless waste; thoughtless, irresponsible exhibitionism. 'Why was this perfume not sold for three hundred denarii', he says, 'and the money given to the poor?' (John 12:5, *NRSV*), and, judged strictly by logic, he has a point. She could indeed have done so much good with the proceeds – wouldn't that have been a better use of resources, an action more pleasing to Jesus? Yet this is to miss the point, for her action symbolises something much deeper: an impulsive spontaneous response, an instinctive gesture of devotion, a heartfelt expression of love. In Jesus she had discovered someone who gave purpose to life, who offered hope, help, meaning, mercy. More than that, through him her brother Lazarus had been brought back to life, summoned from the tomb when all had seemed lost. This wasn't a time for holding back, for weighing up the pros and cons of what to do next; this was a time to pour out her feelings, to let her heart rule her head, to give back to the one who had given so much to her.

That's what it means to love God. Freely and spontaneously to respond to all he has done for us. Is it mere chance that in the words of Deuteronomy we looked at earlier the first instruction is to 'love the Lord your God with all your *heart*'? I don't think so, for it is surely here that love begins. Yes, the mind is important, and, yes, we need to work at the relationship, but that comes second, not first. Above all, faith needs to be an affair of the heart, something that stirs our emotions and captures the imagination.

Yet, if that is one side of love, there is another, for, as we saw earlier, true love involves thinking of one's partner as much as oneself, and striving to live so far as possible in a way that brings them happiness. We see exactly this emphasised in the message of the Old Testament prophets, and, in particular, of Amos and Hosea. Take, for example, the words of the latter concerning what God longs to see from his people: 'I desire steadfast love and not sacrifice, the knowledge of God rather than burnt-offerings' (Hosea 6:6, *NRSV*). The same message is given yet more forcefully in the book of Amos: 'I loathe and reject your festivals, and take no pleasure in your sacred rituals. Bring me your animal sacrifices and cereal offerings if you must – I will not accept them; I want nothing to do with the atoning sacrifices of your fatted animals. Take away from me the clamour of your songs; I will not listen to the tune of your harps. Instead, let justice cascade down like a mighty river, and righteousness like an inexhaustible stream' (Amos 5:21-24). To those on the receiving end of these prophets' words, they must have come like a hammer blow, for they genuinely believed that they loved God. Didn't they faithfully offer him their worship? Were they not scrupulous in their observance of the law? Did they not know the Scriptures back to front? Perhaps they did, but if they imagined that any of this corresponded to loving God they were deluding themselves, for the way they lived ran contrary to his will, flouting everything they knew he desired. So Hosea, borrowing from his own painful experience of a broken marriage, likens Israel to a wanton wife who, though professing loyalty, has been unfaithful to her vows.

We may not outwardly flout God's will in quite the way condemned by these prophets, but we can nonetheless turn faith into a matter of outward observance, superficial show. We do not do it deliberately, but as the first flush of enthusiasm fades, as the cost of discipleship becomes clear, or as familiarity sets in, we can unconsciously settle for compromise, watering down the challenge of the gospel, bending the rules, excusing indiscretions, complacently reassuring ourselves that so long as we say our prayers and share in worship we are doing enough. Does the way we live tally with our claim to love God? Do we strive each day, each moment to do what pleases him? Do we put his will first and our wishes second? Or has our faith become all show with little substance?

'You shall love the Lord your God with all your heart, and with all your soul, and with all your strength' – the words roll off the tongue so easily, don't they? Living by them is another matter, altogether harder. Our love is not perfect, and God doesn't expect it to be, he being the one who took the initiative in establishing a relationship and he the one on whom its future depends, but that's not to say we settle for second best, for half-hearted discipleship. If we truly love God, then we'll seek every day to love him with body, mind and soul – with all our hearts. As the much-loved hymn of Isaac Watts so powerfully puts it:

Were the whole realm of nature mine,
    that were an offering far too small,
    love so amazing, so divine,
    demands my soul, my life, my all.

Summary

- Love involves the heart, the mind, the soul and the will. It needs spontaneity and impulsiveness, but also thoughtfulness and sensitivity towards the wishes of the one loved.

- If that is true in human relationships, it is true also in our relationship with God. As the book of Deuteronomy reminds us, we need to love God with heart, soul, and might. The importance of those words was indelibly printed in the people of Israel from childhood: love of God was placed at the forefront of faith.

- The story of Mary anointing the feet of Jesus with perfume illustrates the need for spontaneity in expressing love. It serves as a model for loving God, which above all needs to involve the heart: a joyful response to all he has done for us.

- By contrast, the words of the prophets Hosea and Amos remind us that love involves our daily actions, that it is no good to say one thing and do another. If the way we live belies our protestations of love, it exposes them as a sham.

- Faith too easily can become a matter of outward observance and religious ritual, divorced from life – a matter of show rather than substance.
- God does not expect our love to be perfect. His love reaches out to us despite our failure to love him as we should, but this should not stop us from giving our best. However flawed our love may be, we need to strive each day to offer God our all.

Discussion

- What do you think it means to love God? What would you say is the most important aspect and how do we most effectively express this?
- Is there a danger of over-emphasising one aspect of loving God at the expense of others – creating a dichotomy perhaps between prayer and action, worship and service?
- Do we dwell too much on faith as an affair of the heart, or, equally, as a matter of intellectual assent? What might cause this? How do we balance the two?
- What things prevent us from loving God as much as we should? In what ways do we need to work at our relationship with God?

Prayer

Sovereign God,
    we say we love you,
    yet all too often the way we live says something else.
We are casual and careless in our relationship with you,
    relegating you to the periphery of life
    instead of placing you at its centre.
We make time for you as an afterthought,

fitting you in as and when the opportunity arises,
and if we cannot find time,
we lose little sleep over the matter.
Our time spent in prayer is erratic,
    our study of your word lackadaisical,
    our commitment half-hearted.
Forgive us for imagining this is sufficient,
    for thinking that our relationship can somehow take care of itself.
Forgive us for loving you so little
    and then wondering why we do not feel as close to you
    as we should.
Teach us what it means to love you with body, mind and soul,
    and help us to be as committed to you as you are to us.
In Christ's name we ask it.
Amen.

Meditation

(*The following meditation explores what it means to love God from the perspective of an ordinary modern-day Christian reflecting on the words of Deuteronomy and the teaching of Jesus concerning love.*)

'You shall love the Lord your God,
    with all your heart,
    all your soul,
    all your mind
    and all your strength.'
I thought I was doing that, Lord –
    I actually believed I was offering total commitment.
When I knelt in prayer,
    sang your praises
    and studied your word,
    it was an act of worship,
    an expression of adoration.
When I brought my gifts,

30

offered my service
and shared my faith,
it was in grateful response,
a declaration of love.
I called it devotion,
and believed it to be just that –
my life consecrated to you –
and it *was* love, so far as it went,
but with all I feel, all I think, all I am? –
I don't think so.
I meant it to be different,
but the love I offered involved just a small part of life,
a prescribed area set aside for you –
spiritual,
sacrosanct –
with the rest lived *my* way,
by *my* rules,
for *my* ends.
Forgive me, Lord,
I don't mean to shut you out;
it's simply that I seldom think to let you in;
but that's the problem:
offering a little of self, so easy,
offering all, so hard.
Yet that's what *you* did –
you gave everything in Christ,
your only Son,
offered freely,
gladly,
without restraint,
your love poured out for many,
I don't get near that,
but I want to try, Lord,
so, by his grace, touch my heart,
and teach me to love you
as you love me.

Further reading: Joshua 23:11

Be very careful to love the Lord your God.

Suggestions for action

Instead of focusing on yourself in prayer, focus on God. As well as offering confession and petition concerned with self, make time for praise and thanksgiving. Build on those prayers, consecrating everything you do each day to God as an expression of all he means to you.

Closing prayer

Gracious God,
    take the little love I have
    and fan it into a mighty flame
    so that I may love you as you deserve,
    to the glory of your name.
Amen.

Third week

Love one another

Opening prayer

O Lord,
   make us to love you
   and each other in you,
   and to meet before you to dwell in your everlasting love,
   through Jesus Christ our Lord.
Amen.

E. B. Pusey (1800; updated)

Introduction

'Let there be love shared among us, let there be love in our eyes.'
So run the opening lines of the popular chorus by David Bilbrough.
Short and simple though it is, it sums up what Christian fellowship
and indeed the gospel itself are ultimately all about, but it's one
thing to sing those words, quite another to apply them in our lives.
The truth is that we find it hard to _like_ some people, let alone _love_
them. Yet running like a refrain throughout the New Testament we
find the challenge to love one another.

What does that mean? How should love show itself? It is
important to avoid sentimentalism here. We are not asked to be
naively idealistic, pretending people are better than they really are,
nor are we expected to ignore their faults and attribute non-existent
virtues. What God does ask, however, is that we genuinely care
about people, looking for the best in them and, as far as possible,
working for their good. Words of Paul to the Philippians capture
the idea well: 'Let each of you look not only to your own interests,
but to the interests of others' (Philippians 2:4, _NRSV_). Such love is

for all, not just the few, but it should find a special place within Christian fellowship, seen above all else as the defining characteristic of the Church. Sadly that is often not so. Few things have the power to divide so much as religion, and Christianity is no exception. All too often, across the years, Christians have been bitterly divided rather than united in Christ, and although ecumenism has helped build many bridges, prejudice and intolerance within various traditions and wings of the Church remain. Within individual fellowships it can be the same story, many racked by differences of opinion or clashes of personality that spill over into suspicion, sniping and even outright hostility. We may be Christians, but we are also all too human, as guilty of the same weaknesses as anyone else. Loving others isn't easy, yet it lies at the heart of our faith, and many will judge us by how far they see it in our lives, whether as individuals or together. What verdict will they reach, I wonder, looking at you and me?

Activity
Pop music quiz (see page 80).

Reading: 1 John 4:7, 11-12
Beloved, let us love one another, because love is from God; everyone who loves is born of God and knows God. Beloved, since God loved us so much, we also ought to love one another. No one has ever seen God; if we love one another, God lives in us, and his love is perfected in us. (NRSV)

Comment

What would you say is your most distinctive feature? Is it a large nose, perhaps, cauliflower ears, a double chin or protruding teeth? Or perhaps it's something more flattering: striking blue eyes, long eyelashes, a fine head of hair, or a rippling muscular physique? Whatever it is, there's almost certainly something that sets you apart, that is unmistakably 'you'. Such features are used to advantage by political cartoonists and satirists. A few deft strokes of the pen, and though the result is an outrageous caricature, we are left in no doubt whom it represents. Similarly, through highlighting a few mannerisms, inflections of the voice or physical characteristics, a gifted impressionist can seemingly conjure up a public figure before our eyes. It seems incredible, but no two people among the countless millions that inhabit our world are exactly alike – there is something distinctive about us all.

What of us as Christians? Is there anything distinctive about our faith, anything that sets us apart and straightaway tells people who we are and what we stand for? If so, what is it? Is moral rectitude the all-important feature, a respectable unblemished lifestyle? Some might suggest so. Is it the fact that we go to church, pray and talk about God? Many non-Christians would probably say just that. Or is the defining characteristic of a Christian something more spiritual: faith that can move mountains, perhaps, or gifts of the Holy Spirit? According to the New Testament, the answer is none of these. Certainly all have their place, or at least they may have in their proper context, but as words of Jesus, the Apostle Paul and the Apostle John make clear, none of them are the be-all and end-all. Indeed, unless they are qualified by an infinitely more important quality they are all but worthless. That quality, of course, is love, and precisely what that means will be the subject of the rest of this book. We will look at loving our enemies, loving our neighbour and loving ourselves, but in this session I want to focus first on the love we are called to share with one another as Christians and with others generally.

One look at the teaching of Jesus leaves us in no doubt that, in his view, love is paramount. 'This is my commandment,' he told his disciples, 'that you love one another as I have loved you' (John 15:12, *NRSV*); words that he amplifies in his final prayer before betrayal and arrest. Although, in the latter, he rarely speaks specifically of loving each other, the idea bubbles below the surface throughout as he speaks of the unity that should characterise the life of God's people, radiating out to others. 'I ask not only on behalf of these, but also of those who will believe in me through their word, that they may all be one . . . I in them and you in me, that they may be completely one, so that the world may know that you have sent me and have loved them even as you have loved me' (John 17:20-21a, 23, *NRSV*). In other words, says Jesus, love, more than anything else, is what will make an impression on others. We can talk as much as we like about other facets of the gospel, but it is the sincerity or otherwise of the love we show for one another that will speak the loudest. This is an idea picked up by Peter Scholtes in his hymn 'We are one in the Spirit', with its closing lines 'And they'll know we are Christians by our love, by our love; yes, they'll know we are Christians by our love.' Is that the case? Is love the quality people associate with Christians? Make no mistake; people will judge the authenticity of our faith by this yardstick more than any other.

In the writings of Paul, Jesus' teaching is expanded and developed, the Apostle leaving us in no doubt that he too considered love to be the distinctive mark of the Christian and hallmark of the Church. Having written of the need for compassion, kindness, humility, meekness, patience and forgiveness, he continues, 'Over all these virtues, put on love, which binds them all together in perfect unity' (Colossians 3:14, *NIV*). Addressed to the church in Colossae, those words were equally applicable to any of the churches he was involved with, the message one that could never be emphasised too much. Then, as now, Christians comprised all kinds of people, inevitably holding contrasting ideas concerning the essentials of faith and discipleship. Despite the rosy picture that is sometimes painted of the early Church, life together was by no means always smooth, a number of bitter disputes over doctrine, the Law and worship frequently leading to controversy and division. On numerous occasions, therefore, Paul had to remind Christians that it isn't outward ritual or doctrinal orthodoxy that holds us together, but the love of Christ. 'Speaking the truth in love, we must grow in every aspect into him, who is the head; that is, into Christ, through whom each part of the body is joined and knitted together by every supporting ligament, so that every part of the body may function as it should, building itself up in love' (Ephesians 4:15-16). His teaching reaches its pinnacle in the unforgettable words of 1 Corinthians 13, a passage that has captured the imagination of Christians and non-Christians alike across the centuries. 'If I speak in the tongues of mortals and of angels, but do not have love, I am a noisy gong or a clanging cymbal. And if I have prophetic powers, and understand all mysteries and all knowledge, and if I have all faith, so as to remove mountains, but do not have love, I am nothing. If I give away all my possessions, and if I hand over my body so that I may boast, but do not have love, I gain nothing. Love is patient; love is kind; love is not envious or boastful or arrogant or rude. It does not insist on its own way; it is not irritable or resentful; it does not rejoice in wrongdoing, but rejoices in the truth. It bears all things, believes all things, hopes all things, endures all things' (1 Corinthians 13:1-7, *NRSV*).

Finally, we turn to the words of our reading from the first Epistle of John. The language here may be less memorable than Paul's, but it is equally forthright, if not more so, the importance of love as *the* essential criterion of faith uncompromisingly spelt out. 'Beloved, let us love one another, because love comes from God; everyone who loves is born of God and knows God. Those who say, "I love God," and hate their brothers or sisters, are liars; for those who do not love a brother or sister whom they have seen, cannot love God whom they have not seen. The commandment we have from him is this: those who love God must love their brothers and sisters also' (1 John 4:7, 20-21, *NRSV*). The message could not be more clear: love is not an optional extra, an appendage to discipleship – it *is* discipleship. Unless we love one another we do not and cannot love God – the truth is that simple. On the one hand, that is a wonderfully liberating message, for it clears away all the clutter that sometimes obscures the heart of the gospel. On the other hand, it is almost frightening, for few of us find love easy.

In what ways, then, do we need to love one another? To discuss that fully would take far longer than a brief session such as this, but let me point to three areas that might repay further thought. Firstly, we need to develop an attitude that believes the best, not just in our relationships with other Christians but with everybody. That is not to say we encourage naiveté, to suggest that we should view people through rose-coloured spectacles minimising their faults or exaggerating their virtues. Far from it, we need to be realistic in our appraisal, fully aware of the evil some are capable of and the faults we all suffer from. The difference is that love does not give up on people; it refuses to dismiss them as worthless and consign them to the refuse tip. However much *we* may struggle to see anything of worth in some individuals, *God* sees a person of infinite worth, someone he values enough to die for. On occasions, we may struggle to accept that, yet that is the stark challenge of the gospel. In terms of Christian fellowship, of course, we will rarely come up against overt evil, but the same principle applies and more so. The person who rubs us up the wrong way, who seems to disagree with us at every turn, who comes across as narrow, intolerant, judgemental, or whatever it may be – they are still part of our family in Christ; important to God and in consequence important to us. They may be weak and human, but so are we. They may make mistakes, but don't we do the same? They may not be perfect, but are any of us? In all our relationships, whoever we are talking about, we need to cultivate the love Paul speaks of that 'bears all things, believes all things, hopes all things, endures all things'.

In a sense, that says it all, but we need to work out what this means in practice. Is there somebody in your church facing difficulties; unwell, perhaps, infirm, depressed, housebound, lonely? What are you doing to show your concern, your love for them? It needn't be much, but a phone call, a card, a visit, a friendly word can mean so much, assuring the individual in question that they are not alone, that someone cares. Of course, we need to be sensitive, aware that our presence at times may not be wanted or needed, but that should not stop us from making the initial approach, so long as our love is sincere. Don't wait for someone else to do it; consider what you might be able to do to lighten another's load.

Finally, we need to consider our attitude to Christians whose convictions or expression of faith differ from our own. In part, that means our relationships with those of other denominations. Great strides have been made in terms of Christian unity, and members of churches representing diverse traditions worship together in a way that would have seemed unthinkable 30 or 40 years ago, though at times progress may be more apparent than real. Many are still suspicious of or even hostile towards certain denominations, accepting them on sufferance if at all. Many more only meet other Christians once or twice each year; at a United Service perhaps in the Week of Prayer for Christian Unity, or at a shared Good Friday or Christmas service. Only the enthusiastic few participate in Lent study groups, while still less support inter-church community initiatives. Have we truly learned what it means to love one another in the community of faith, in such a way that those outside can see we are Christians by our love?

If denominationalism is still an issue, however, a far greater one is the divide between styles of worship that we might loosely label charismatic and traditional – a divide that includes, in varying degrees, disagreements concerning theology, worship and church practice. Some speak dismissively of 'dead' churches, others mutter concerning the 'happy-clappy brigade'; on both sides derogatory labels are bandied about that enable people to dispense with the need for considered reflection or openness to new ideas. The painful experience of schism in innumerable churches up and down the country bears stark testimony to the heat such differences can generate. Of course some of us will feel happier with one way of worship than another. Of course there will be contrasting emphases in our understanding of God. Of course the way we express our faith will reflect our individual temperaments and personalities. And, yes, that will inevitably sometimes mean groups of likeminded people coming together while others go elsewhere, but does that need to lead to judgemental attitudes, rejection, bitterness, even animosity? If so, what then of our claim to love one another?

We talk a lot in the Church about love, and we're right to, for without it faith is indeed nothing. That, though, begs the question: do we show it? It's not simply a matter of loving other Christians – God forbid! It involves, as we shall see in our final three sessions, love for those outside the Church as well as for ourselves, but if we fail to show it to those with whom we share faith in Christ, what hope is there of showing it to anyone else? We can't make it happen ourselves; we need God's love to flow within us, each of us each day opening ourselves to his grace. In the words of the well-known hymn, we need to pray, 'Bind us together, Lord, bind us together with cords that cannot be broken; bind us together in love', for it is only with his help that we can become the people he wants us to be.

Summary

- Just as every individual has certain distinguishing features, so we as Christians should have something that sets us apart.
- Of all the qualities we might come up with, none is more important than love. Without this, all else is nothing.
- Jesus gave one new commandment to his followers: to love one another. Both here, and in his 'high-priestly' prayer of John 17, he made it clear that love should be the quality that characterises the Church, speaking to those outside it of the truth of the gospel.
- Similarly, Paul, in several of his letters, spoke of the importance of love, emphasising that this is what ties everything together. Nowhere is his teaching more memorably expressed than in the words of 1 Corinthians 13.
- In the first Epistle of John, the importance of loving one another is spelt out in uncompromising terms as the hallmark of true

faith. If such love is lacking, John tells us, then we do not truly love God.

- In general terms, we need to love in the sense of believing the best of others, not in the sense of glossing over their faults but in believing they are still of value. Just as God refuses to write them off, neither can we.

- We need to consider practical steps we can take to express love in action. Through sensitively responding in small but simple ways to needs within our own fellowship, we can make our talk about love real.

- Our love for one another should span denominational divides and differences concerning worship or theology. While we will all have our own personal convictions and ways of expressing our faith, we need to do that in a spirit of love and mutual respect.

- Loving others involves all, including ourselves, but if we cannot love our fellow Christians it bodes ill for loving anyone else. We need to ask God each day to bind us together in love.

Discussion

- How far is love the motivating factor behind our actions? What other factors might get in the way of love?

- Would anyone know you are a Christian by your love? What do you find hardest about loving?

- In what ways can we express love for one another? In what ways do we fail to do so? What concrete steps can we take to translate words into deeds?

Prayer

Lord Jesus Christ,
    you summed up the law in one simple word: 'love'.
Forgive us that, though we often talk about love,
    we rarely show it in practice.
Forgive us everything in our lives that denies love:
    the angry words and unkind comments;
    the thoughtless deeds and careless actions;
    the sorrow we have brought rather than joy,
    and hurt rather than healing;
    the care we have failed to express,
    support we have refused to offer
    and forgiveness we have been unwilling to extend.
Help us to look to you who showed love in action –
    a love that bears all things,
    believes all things,
    hopes all things,
    endures all things –
    and help us truly to realise that unless such love flows within us
    all our words, faith and religion count for nothing.
Teach us, then, to love one another,
    as you have loved us.
Amen.

Meditation

(*What does it mean to love others, and have we sufficient strength to do it? Most of us want to love others better, but we find it hard to put their needs before our own. This meditation, taking the form of a question and answer in prayer, explores the nature of truly sacrificial love, and reminds us that God displayed just this through the suffering and death of Jesus. It is in experiencing his love that we are set free to love others in turn.*)

Lord, I saw a photograph today,
    a picture of a mother desperately shielding her baby

from a hail of bullets,
    sacrificing herself to protect her little one.
And there I saw love,
    total love –
    not the pale imitation we pass off in its place,
    but the real thing,
    concerned only to give,
    pouring itself out, oblivious to the cost.
I admired that, Lord,
    and I longed to share it.
No, not the pain and sacrifice, not that,
    but the ability to love
    with even a fraction of that selfless devotion –
    for I know deep down that I don't.
I speak of love often enough –
    sign off with it in a letter,
    send it casually over the phone –
    but it's just a word,
    well-intentioned but hollow.
And even with those dearest to me,
    my friends and family,
    though I care deeply about them, more than they will ever know,
    my love is still imperfect,
    as much about *me* as them –
    my happiness,
    my desires,
    my wishes,
    my well-being.
I'm not good at loving, Lord,
    and that troubles me, for it strikes at the very heart of my faith.
Love your enemy,
    love your neighbour,
    love one another –
    isn't that what you tell us to do?
And it all sounds wonderful,
    a recipe for heaven.

But it's one thing to bandy such fine words as theory –
  I do it all the time –
  it's another to mean them, let alone to make them real.

My child,
  it's quite true what you say –
  love *is* difficult,
  more costly and demanding than most people ever imagine;
  and it's true also that your love is less than it ought to be,
  as much about yourself as others.
But that's not so terrible,
  for I tell you this, unless you learn to love self
  you will never love anyone else.
Besides, there is more to you than you give credit for.
That picture you speak of, the mother shielding her child –
  you're not so different, despite what you think.
You too could rise to that same devotion and commitment,
  that same willingness to sacrifice all.
It would take a lot, I grant you,
  and I hope you'll never be put to the test,
  but there are those you care about enough
  to die for them if necessary.
Believe me, I know,
  for I care that much about you, about everyone;
  only it cost me more still –
  the cruellest of agonies,
  the most unimaginable pain.
I came to this world in Jesus,
  sharing your human suffering,
  bearing your grief and sorrow,
  and out of love I watched him give everything,
  nailed to the cross so that you might live.
It was dreadful,
  harder than you will ever know not to step in and call a halt –
  my child far too precious to die like that.
But I held back, honouring his wishes,

as he laid down his life for all.
So, yes, it's difficult – love – I understand that,
    but it's not impossible, not now anyway,
    for it's been given freely, in the blood of my Son shed for you –
    and when love like that flows through your veins
    it must surely soon beat in your heart.

Further reading: 1 John 3:23

This is his commandment, that we should believe in the name of his Son Jesus Christ and love one another, just as he has commanded us. (*NRSV*)

Suggestions for action

Do something this week to express your love for other Christians. If someone in your fellowship is unwell, for example, why not send a card, ring or call in to visit. If there are those in your fellowship whom you do not know very well, make a point of talking to them, particularly those whose emphasis in theology or worship might be different from your own. Or why not visit a church of another denomination, and recognise the unity you share in Christ with all his people?

Closing prayer

Gracious God,
    take the little love we have.
Nurture, deepen and expand it,
    until we have learned what love really means,
    until your love flows through in our hearts,
    until love is all in all.
Through Jesus Christ our Lord.
Amen.

Fourth week

Love your enemies

Opening prayer

O holy and ever-blessed Lord,
> teach us, we pray, to love one another,
> to exercise forbearance and forgiveness towards our enemies,
> to recompense no one evil for evil,
> but to be merciful even as you, our Father in heaven, are merciful;
> so that we may continually follow after you in all our doings,
> and be more and more conformed to your image and likeness,
> through Jesus Christ our Lord.

Amen.

Taken from New Book of Worship _(1876; updated)_

Introduction

'We'll never forgive him as long as we live!' I well understood the couple's bitterness, for their child had been left permanently brain-damaged through a doctor's misdiagnosis. Had I been in their shoes, I'd have felt just the same. It's hard to forgive those whose actions cause us hurt or injure our loved ones. In this case, the object of their anger wasn't an enemy but someone who had made a genuine mistake. How much harder it must be to forgive those who purposely maim, wound or destroy. To love our enemies sounds wonderful in theory, but it is all too easy to be precious about it, spouting fine-sounding rhetoric from the sidelines. Few of us, if put on the spot, would rise above bitterness and hatred. The tragedy is that those very feelings are as destructive as any physical injury, suffocating and poisoning the spirit deep within.

Can we love our enemies? What does that mean? We find it

hard enough to forgive our friends when they cause us hurt, let alone our enemies. Many of us, I suspect, have wrestled uncomfortably with these demanding words of Jesus and then thrust them to the back of our minds, hoping they will go away. That may be the easiest option, but it is not the way of Christ. Like it or not, he calls us to love all people, both good and evil. I struggle with that concept as much as any, yet if we are serious about discipleship, we have to come to terms with it. There are no easy answers, but that doesn't mean we can duck the question.

Activity
Enemies quiz (see page 80).

Reading: Matthew 5:43-46
You have heard that it was said, 'You shall love your neighbour and hate your enemy.' But I tell you, love your enemies and pray for those who persecute you, so that you may become children of your Father in heaven; for he causes his sun to rise on the evil and the good, and the rain to fall on the just and the unjust. What's so special about loving those who love you? Even tax collectors manage that.

Comment
The theme of this session – love your enemies – is one that I find difficult. Why? Because I doubt my ability to do what it asks. Thankfully, so far as I'm aware, I have no enemies, but what if I had? Could I love them? Perhaps I could if they merely didn't like me, but if they wished me harm or, worse still, harmed my loved ones, could I love them then? It would be incredibly hard. Imagine what it must have been like to be a Jew in occupied Europe during

the Holocaust, shepherded into the gas chambers or starving in concentration camps. Could you have loved the Nazis? Imagine being a Muslim in Bosnia during the horrific days of 'ethnic cleansing'. Could you have loved the Serbs? Imagine yourself in Cambodia during the tyrannical years of Pol Pot. Could you have loved the killing squads that roamed the countryside indiscriminately massacring men, women and children alike? I honestly don't think I could. Indeed, it seems ridiculous even to suggest it.

Part of the problem, of course, as we shall explore later, lies in our understanding of the word 'love'. If we take it to mean anything approximating to affection, then in the contexts I've outlined above it is clearly absurd. Yet giving way to hatred seems equally unacceptable for that is an emotion which consumes the one who hates as much as the one hated, eating away and destroying from within. Worse still, it sets up a vicious circle, breeding further hatred with everything associated with that. Look at the troubled history of Northern Ireland across the years, one murder inevitably leading to another in tit-for-tat killings. It took the voices of those willing to forgive, such as Gordon Wilson in his unforgettable response to the Enniskillen bomb blast, to break the cycle of slaughter and pave the way for the recent peace process, but such is the ingrained suspicion and hostility bred by the years of hatred that the progress of this initiative has been slow and unsteady. Even this, though, is as nothing compared to the situation in the Middle East, where long-standing enmity between Israel and Palestine has recently exploded into unprecedented carnage. To the outsider, it is clear that the only solution to that conflict lies in letting go of the past and putting old grievances aside. To those, however, who have seen loved ones killed in a suicide bombing, shot by snipers or killed in a revenge attack, it is a very different matter.

Is it possible to love our enemies? I want to look briefly at three people who did just that. The first comes from the Old Testament, in the person of David. Initially a favourite of King Saul, relationships between the two of them soured as Saul's jealousy over David's exploits in battle took hold. When cheering crowds sang of Saul killing his thousands but David his ten thousands, 'Saul eyed

David from that day on' (1 Samuel 18:9, *NRSV*), and when it became clear to Saul that God's favour rested on his rival, 'Saul was David's enemy from that time forward' (1 Samuel 18:29, *NRSV*). There followed repeated attempts on David's life, and life as a renegade in the wilderness, hunted down like a wild animal. Yet, through it all, David refused to give in to hatred. When Saul inadvertently blundered into a cave where he was sheltering, David spurned the opportunity to kill him, much to Saul's amazement: 'who has ever found an enemy, and sent the enemy safely away?' (1 Samuel 24:19a, *NRSV*). Similar incidents were to follow, David not only refusing to harm Saul but also being ready to forgive and forget. When news finally reached him of Saul's death in battle his response was not one of relief and celebration but genuine sorrow. We cannot push this example too far, for David held no love for most of his enemies, as witnessed in his encounter with Goliath, but amid the brutality of war and conquest we glimpse here a different perspective – one that anticipates, at least in part, the subsequent message of the gospel.

It is that message which shines from our second example: Stephen, the first Christian martyr. Appointed by the Apostles to share in the practical work of the Church, he swiftly made an impact through his life and witness, but his ministry had scarcely begun before he was seized by the Jewish authorities, accused of blasphemy, and condemned to death by stoning. It must have been an agonising and dreadful way to die, yet, we read, 'as they stoned him . . . he knelt down and called out, "Lord, do not hold this sin against them"' (Acts 7:59a, 60). Here was the ultimate act of forgiveness – pardoning one's killers – and it leads us, of course, to our third example, that of Jesus himself.

'Father, forgive them; for they do not know what they are doing' (Luke 23:34, *NRSV*). We know those words so well that their impact is not perhaps what it once was, yet they exemplify the way of forgiveness, what it means to love one's enemies. Here was Jesus, the paradigm of love, blameless of any wrongdoing, done to death, the victim of fear, pride, expediency, hatred and misunderstanding, yet his concern was not for himself but his killers; for all those, us included, who in some way were responsible for his death. 'Love your enemies and pray for those who persecute you,' he had said, and there on the cross he did precisely that.

Does it take a special sort of person to show such love? I think it does, but this shouldn't stop us from trying to emulate their example as best we can. Thankfully, few of us have enemies who wish us physical harm, yet people can still bring us pain, wounding us through unkind words, sniping through insinuations, causing hurt whenever and wherever the opportunity presents itself. They may be colleagues at work, resentful perhaps of our success or hostile to faith. They may be those with whom there is a clash of personality, temperaments or characters. They may be problem neighbours, rivals in love, or bullies at school. For others, the challenge is greater: victims of racial abuse and discrimination, of crime, violence, sexual harassment and so on. For us all there is also a broader canvas, in the form of extremism, terrorism and anarchy in an ever more destabilised world. It was rightly said by many that 11 September 2001 changed the world for ever, the perceptions of many having radically and irrevocably altered. Can we and should we talk about loving our enemies in this context?

We need to remember that we are not talking here about love in a romantic or idealised sense – about liking people or pretending they are something they are not. Understood in this way, loving our enemies is patently unrealistic, out of touch with the facts. No, we are talking about something very different: recognising the evil people are capable of yet seeking their good; enduring what they might throw at us yet being ready to forgive; experiencing the worst yet still looking for the best in them. It means refusing to meet hatred with hatred, rejecting 'an eye for an eye and a tooth for a tooth', and instead turning the other cheek, striving to conquer evil with good and hate with love. Can you do that? I'm still not sure I can. Indeed, I'm not sure what such love might involve or how we begin to work it out in practice. Yet, having said that, I believe we need to try, for one look at our world today, with its continuing tensions and conflicts, violence and division, prejudice and intolerance, gives us a bleak picture of the alternative.

Summary

- When we put ourselves in the shoes of many across the years, it is hard to imagine we could ever love our enemies. In many situations, love in the sense of feeling liking or affection is clearly absurd.
- Hatred, however, breeds further hatred, leading to an escalating spiral. It needs someone with the courage to show love and forgiveness if the cycle is to be broken.
- In David's dealings with Saul, we see an early, albeit limited, example of loving one's enemy.
- In Stephen, we see someone who followed in the footsteps of Christ, forgiving his killers as they stoned him to death for his faith.
- Jesus didn't simply speak of loving one's enemies; he acted upon his words, asking God's forgiveness for those responsible for his death.
- Few of us have enemies who wish us actual harm, but they can still cause us emotional hurt. Are we willing and ready to forgive and love them?
- Others in our society face more concrete threats. For them the challenge is more acute.
- Growing religious, political and cultural polarisation in the international arena brings with it new tensions and raises complex practical and ethical questions concerning who is our enemy and how we respond to them.
- Loving our enemies doesn't mean liking them or feeling affection. It means rather meeting hatred with love, and striving to overcome evil with good. We need to wrestle with the implications of what that means in our world today.

Discussion

- In what ways does the challenge to love our enemies apply to us today? Are we simply talking hypothetically, or have we come up against those we might call enemies?
- What things would we find hard, if not impossible, to forgive? Who would we correspondingly find it difficult to love?
- How far is it realistic to meet hatred with love and evil with good? Are there not times when violence has to be met with violence, such as in the Second World War or international intervention in Kosovo? What yardstick do we use to judge when such action is justified? How do we relate this to our faith?
- Could we love our enemies without the safety net of effective policing and a legal system administering justice and punishment? In what way does a desire for justice differ from a desire for vengeance?

Prayer

Lord,
>we are told that the strongest survive,
>that in this world it's a question of never mind the rest
>so long as we're all right.

Yet, you call us to another way –
>the way of humility, sacrifice and self-denial.

You stand accepted wisdom on its head,
>claiming that the meek shall inherit the earth
>and that those who are willing to lose their lives
>will truly find them.

Lord,
>it is hard to believe in this way of yours,
>and harder still to live by it,
>for it runs contrary to everything we know about human nature;
>yet we have seen for ourselves that the world's way
>leads so often to hurt, sorrow and division.

Give us faith and courage, then,
  to live out the foolishness of the gospel,
  and so to bring closer the kingdom of Christ, here on earth.
In his name we ask it.
  Amen.

Meditation of a listener to the Sermon on the Mount

Can you believe what he told us?
Love your enemies, that's what he said!
Pray for those who abuse you,
  and if someone slaps you in the face, turn the other cheek!
Well, I ask you, what sort of talk is that?
He's on another planet, this fellow –
  cloud-cuckoo land!
Oh it sounds wonderful, granted,
  but can you see it working?
I can't.
No, we have to be sensible about these things,
  realistic.
We'd all like the world to be different,
  but it's no use pretending, is it?
'Love your enemies' –
  where will that get us?
They'll see us coming a mile off!
And as for 'turn the other cheek' –
  well, *you* can if you want to, but not me;
  I'll give them one back with interest –
  either that or run for it!
I'll tell you what, though,
  we listened to him,
  all of us,
  just about the biggest crowd I've ever seen
  hanging on to his every word,
  listening like I've rarely known people listen before.

Why?
Well, you could see he meant what he was saying for one thing –
    the way he handled the hecklers and cynics:
    never losing his cool,
    never lashing out in frustration,
    ready to suffer for his convictions if that's what it took.
He practised what he preached,
    and there aren't many you can say that about, are there?
But it was more than that.
Like it or not, it was his message itself;
    that crazy message
    so different from any we'd ever heard before –
    impractical,
    unworkable,
    yet irresistible.
It gave us a glimpse of the way life could be,
    the way it should be –
    and he actually made us feel that one day it might be!
No, I'm not convinced, sad to say –
    life's just not like that –
    but I wish it was.
I wish I had the courage to try his way,
    the faith to give it a go,
    for we've been trying the way of the world
    for as long as I can remember,
    and look where that's got us!

Further reading: Luke 6:27-28

I say to all who are willing to listen, 'Love your enemies, do good to those who hate you, bless those who curse you and pray for those who abuse you.'

Suggestions for action

Pray for anyone against whom you hold a grievance or who has caused you hurt. If possible, and practical, take steps to show love and acceptance.

Closing prayer

Gracious God,
    teach me the secret of a love that goes on loving,
    despite all it faces.
Through Jesus Christ my Lord.
Amen.

Fifth week

Love your neighbour

Opening prayer

O Lord,
   who, though you were rich, yet for our sakes became poor,
   and who promised in your gospel that whatever is done
   to the least of your brothers and sisters,
   you will receive as done for you;
   give us grace, we humbly ask,
   to be ever willing and ready to minister, as you enable us,
   to the needs of our fellow human beings,
   and to extend the blessings of your kingdom over all the world,
   to your praise and glory,
   God over all,
   blessed for ever.
Amen.

St Augustine (updated)

Introduction

The whole law encapsulated in two commandments revolving around one word: love – it all sounds so easy, doesn't it, so wonderfully straightforward. Or at least it does until we realise who our neighbours are. According to the parable of the good Samaritan, they are not just those who live next door or nearby, but everyone, everywhere! No person is outside our concern, no situation one that we can wash our hands of.

We cannot, of course, respond to all who are in need, and I don't for a moment expect that Jesus intends us to, but how far do we respond to any? A second parable – that of the sheep and the goats – indicates that practical service is the decisive test of commitment. It is, then, no accident that the need to love both God and our neighbour is mentioned in the same breath. Faith, in part, is about God's love for us and ours for him, but unless that love embraces also our neighbour, then it is not love at all.

Activity
Neighbours quiz (see page 81).

Reading: Luke 10:25-37
Just then a lawyer stood up to test Jesus. 'Teacher,' he said, 'what must I do to inherit eternal life?' He said to him, 'What is written in the law? What do you read there?' He answered, 'You shall love the Lord your God with all your heart, and with all your soul, and with all your strength, and with all your mind; and your neighbour as yourself.' And he said to him, 'You have given the right answer; do this, and you will live.'

But wanting to justify himself, he asked Jesus, 'And who is my neighbour?' Jesus replied, 'A man was going down from Jerusalem to Jericho, and fell into the hands of robbers, who stripped him, beat him, and went away, leaving him half dead. Now by chance a priest was going down that road; and when he saw him, he passed by on the other side. So likewise a Levite, when he came to the place and saw him, passed by on the other side. But a Samaritan while travelling came near him; and when he saw him, he was moved with pity. He went to him and bandaged his wounds, having poured oil and wine on them. Then he put him on his own animal, brought him to an inn, and took care of him. The next day he took out two denarii, gave them to the innkeeper, and said, "Take care of him; and when I come back, I will repay you whatever more you spend." Which of these three, do you think, was a neighbour to the man who fell into the hands of the robbers?' He said, 'The one who showed him mercy.' Jesus said to him, 'Go and do likewise.' (*NRSV*)

Comment

The sign was bold and unmistakable, informing all who passed by that they were entering a Neighbourhood Watch area, and I immediately felt self-conscious, certain that numerous eyes were fastened upon me wondering what such a shady individual was doing walking down their street. Hopefully, potential crooks will feel the same, for that, of course, is the purpose of the scheme – to provide an effective deterrent against crime. Since its launch 20 years ago, Neighbourhood Watch has been an enormous success, offering residents across the country the opportunity to participate in ensuring the security of their local community, or, in other words, to play their part as neighbours. This is not the only way, of course, that neighbourliness can be expressed. A variety of 'good neighbour' schemes have proliferated over recent years, affording people the opportunity to offer practical assistance to others, particularly those suffering deprivation. In addition, a host of ordinary individuals provide help to elderly, infirm or housebound neighbours in numerous small but simple ways. It is often in this way, through serving the local community, that Christian convictions can most effectively be worked out in practice, our talk of love and compassion translated into concrete action. This can either be as part of a co-ordinated church programme – a fellowship wanting to express its on-going commitment to the community in which it is set – or through individuals showing such concern on their own initiative, without any overtly Christian agenda. It makes no difference – a simple act of love towards our neighbour can be as meaningful an expression of Christian commitment as any other, as Jesus' parable of the sheep and goats makes plain. In any discussion of loving our neighbour, then, we need to ask first, do we offer as much help as we are able to those we might term our neighbours in the established sense of the word? If there is a local need we can respond to, some practical way in which we can express Christ's love for others, do we take it, or is ours a faith strong on religion but weak on service, hot on personal spirituality but cool on serving others, long on selfishness but short on love? On one level, when Jesus talked of loving our neighbour he meant just that – the gospel begins down our street.

All right, we might say, I can manage that, just about. Unfortunately, though, that's not the end of the story. It may have been once in the days before high-speed travel, television, telephone and the Internet, but we live today in a different world, a world much smaller than it has ever been before. We can travel across the globe in a matter of hours and even venture into space. We can watch events live by satellite from thousands of miles, and items of news reach our homes from every country almost as they happen. We can talk on the phone or online to people in distant continents almost as if they are in our own front room. Today, as never before, the furthest corners of the earth are accessible to us at the push of a button or flick of a switch. That fact brings enormous blessings but also new responsibilities and demands. 'Who is my neighbour?' the lawyer asked Jesus (Luke 10:29). Where does love begin and end? And in truth he didn't seriously expect an answer. This was a question designed to embarrass Jesus, to show that all his talk about compassion for the poor, acceptance of strangers and love for one's neighbour was idealistic empty nonsense – nice in theory but not part of the real world. Yet Jesus, of course, through the parable of the good Samaritan, turns the question back on the questioner. 'Which of these,' he says, 'was a neighbour to the man?' And suddenly the answer to the lawyer's question becomes clear: a neighbour is anyone and everyone in need.

Two thousand years ago that challenge must have seemed daunting enough; today it is massive, for suddenly every person in every country has become our concern; every disaster our disaster; every*one* our neighbour. When floods strike Bangladesh, we know; when famine hits Sudan, we know; when students are massacred in Tiananmen Square, we know. Day after day, pictures of emaciated children confront us as we sit down to our meal of plenty; of the homeless as we sit in the warmth and comfort of our homes; of the poor as we enjoy an ever-rising standard of living. All these are our neighbours in today's small world. Whether we like it or not, they span the globe, from Africa to India, from those living down our street to those in the shantytowns of Brazil. Charity may still begin at home, but it cannot end there.

By ourselves, of course, we cannot put all the world's ills to right, nor respond to every place of need, but neither can we turn our backs and pretend that they are none of our business. At times we may feel overwhelmed by the scale of the challenge. How can we continue giving when our own resources are already stretched? How can we pray meaningfully or effectively when there are so many people in need? How can we seriously expect to make a difference in the face of global economic realities? Yet respond we must, not out of duty or guilt, but because that is what Christ would have done and what he calls us to do; because through responding to them we respond to Christ himself. '"I was hungry and you gave me something to eat, thirsty and you gave me a drink, a stranger and you made me welcome, naked and you clothed me, sick and you visited me, in prison and you had time for me." Then the righteous will answer, "Lord, when did we see you hungry and give you food, or thirsty and give you a drink? When did we see you a stranger and make you welcome, or naked and clothe you? When was it that we saw you sick or in prison and visited you?" Then the king will answer, "I tell you the truth, whenever you did it to the least of your brothers and sisters, you did it also to me"' (Matthew 25:35-40).

There is more, though, to the parable of the good Samaritan than simply responding to the needy. At its heart is the fact that the one who offered help was a Samaritan; in other words, a sworn enemy of the Jews. A respectable Jew would do everything possible to avoid contact with such a person, just as a Samaritan would make every effort to keep well away from any Jew. Yet this Samaritan was different. He saw beyond the artificial barriers we construct to the person behind, recognising that our common humanity surpasses anything that may divide us. Similar barriers have manifested themselves since in apartheid, the Iron Curtain, ethnic cleansing and the like, but equally they find a place in our own lives. Are we open to meeting our neighbour in anyone and everyone, irrespective of class, colour, culture or creed? We may think so, but how do we really feel about those different to ourselves? For all the changes of recent years, the world is as divided today as it has ever been, prejudice and intolerance dividing person from person, country from country, and faith from faith. In the wake of the cataclysmic events in New York on 11 September 2001, there is a risk of those divisions growing ever wider, mistrust between the Muslim and Christian worlds reaching dangerous new heights. Unless we learn to live as neighbours, open to giving and receiving, and engaging in genuine dialogue, the future for world peace and security looks bleak.

The parable of the good Samaritan contains a sting in the tail that we may sometimes overlook. Which of the three travellers failed to help the man set upon by bandits? It was, of course, the priest and the Levite, both passing by on the other side. In other words, it was religious people, those convinced they were doing everything God could ask and a good deal more besides. If anyone should have stopped and offered help, it was them, for they claimed to understand and honour God's will better than anyone. If anyone should have been open to others, it was them, for did they not believe that God was ultimately God of all? The truth is, however, that they were so wrapped up in themselves, in their own little worlds, that they failed to see and respond to a fellow human being right under their noses. Don't let that be true of us. Don't let us turn so much in on ourselves that we forget about others. Personal devotion, worship and celebration are all important in expressing our love for God, as too are sharing fellowship and sharing our faith, but the teaching of Jesus makes clear that loving our neighbour is equally important – perhaps most important of all.

Summary

- People today can act as good neighbours in numerous ways. A host of avenues for service offer the ideal opportunity to express Christian commitment in action.

- Our neighbours, however, are not simply those who live in our street or town. Thanks to modern technology and associated developments in communication, we are part of a small world in which everyone has become our neighbour. As Christians, we must respond to them as well as to those closer to home.

- On one level, the parable of the good Samaritan challenges us concerning our response to the needy of our world. The scale of that challenge may sometimes seem overwhelming, yet we need to do what we can. None of us can do everything alone, but we must all play our part. As the parable of the sheep and the goats makes clear, through responding to others we respond to Christ himself, and if we fail one we fail in both.

- The good Samaritan is also a parable about breaking down barriers. It challenges us on a second level concerning our openness to others of different countries, colours, cultures and creeds to our own. In a world of escalating divisions, we need to learn to live as neighbours, and that begins in our own relationships.

- We must beware of becoming so wrapped up in church activities or in our personal relationship with God that we forget our responsibility towards our neighbours. Love of God and our neighbour should always go hand in hand.

Discussion

- In what ways can we extend love to our neighbour today? What avenues for service are there within our local community? What things hold us back from supporting these? Are there needs in our neighbourhood not being met? Can we do anything about them?

- In what ways are we closed to others? What are the things in today's world that most divide people? How much are we influenced by these?
- How far does neighbourliness extend? Do we sometimes neglect the wider world, arguing that charity begins at home, or is the problem the other way round?
- Is there a danger of becoming so involved in church activities that we limit our involvement in and concern for the world outside? Can the church become overly introspective, too concerned with *religion* and not concerned enough with serving the community? Do we need a balance between attending church committees, meetings and activities, and encouraging people to be active in the *real world*?

Prayer

Lord Jesus Christ.
  your words concerning love for our neighbour
  sound so wonderful
  until we stop to ask what they mean,
  and then, suddenly, the scale of the challenge,
  the enormity of our responsibility
  and the likely cost of service dawns on us
  and we wonder how we can ever begin to respond.
Teach us that, though we can't do everything,
  we can do something.
Teach us that a little offered in faith can achieve much by your grace.
Fill us, then, with your love so that we may love in turn,
  and in serving others may we also serve you,
    to the glory of your name.
Amen.

Meditation of the lawyer who questioned Jesus

'Teacher,' I said, 'what must I do to inherit eternal life?'
I knew what he was going to say, even as I put the question.
It was typical of the man's genius,
    somehow always turning the tables
    on those who tried to catch him out.
And this time was no exception.
'What is written in the law?' he asked. 'What do you read there?'
Brilliant!
Only this time he would meet his match,
    for, unlike others, I was ready for him,
    all set to turn the tables back again
    and put him firmly on the spot.
So I played along, confident of emerging on top.
'Love God,' I said, 'love your neighbour.'
It was the answer he'd been looking for,
    and he nodded with a smile of satisfaction,
    as though that was that,
    the discussion at an end,
    the issue resolved:
    'Do this and you will live.'
But that was my cue,
    and I leapt in gleefully,
    sensing the kill.
'Yes,' I smirked, 'but who is my neighbour?'
Clever, don't you think?
And I genuinely believed I had him stumped,
    one masterly stroke exposing the fatal flaw in his reasoning.
You see it sounds reasonable enough, doesn't it? –
    'love your neighbour as yourself':
    the sort of commandment none of us would want to argue with,
    never even presume to question –
    but what does it actually mean?
If you've never asked yourself that, then it's high time you did,
    for perhaps then you'd be a little less keen on the idea,

a little less prone to let the words trip so lightly off the tongue.
Why?
Well, quite simply, how wide do you spread the net?
How far do you go before finally drawing the line?
The people next door, are they your neighbours?
Or is it those in your street, your town, your country,
    those who share your creed, or colour, or culture?
Where does it start?
Where does it end?
You tell me.
And that's the question I put to Jesus,
    fully expecting him to flounder
    as he tried to extricate himself from my trap.
Come on, I reasoned, there had to be limits somewhere!
The Romans, for example,
    our hated oppressors –
    he couldn't mean them for a start.
Nor tax-collectors, prostitutes and sinners,
    you could write them off for certain –
    accept them and we'd be talking of Samaritans next, God forbid!
And what of our enemies,
    those who persecute, insult and accuse us falsely –
    don't tell me we're meant to love them too?
Preposterous!
No, I had him pinned down,
    his back to the wall,
    and there could surely be no escape.
Only then he looked at me,
    and told that unforgettable story about,
    you've guessed it . . . a *Samaritan*! –
    and somehow the question was once again back where it started,
    with *me*:
    'Which of these three was a neighbour to the man?'
I realised then with a stab of shock
    and a sense of disbelief,
    that he meant it,

that he seriously wants us to treat everyone, everywhere,
   as our neighbour,
   Jew and Gentile,
   slave and free,
   male and female,
   rich and poor –
no person outside our concern,
no situation we can wash our hands of.
I'd put the question,
   I'd had my answer,
   and, I tell you what,
   I wish I'd never asked!

Further reading: Romans 13:8-10

Owe no one anything, except to love one another, for the one who loves another has fulfilled the law. The commandments, 'You shall not commit adultery; You shall not murder; You shall not steal; You shall not covet'; and any other commandment, are summed up in this word, 'Love your neighbour as yourself.' Love does no wrong to a neighbour; therefore, love is the fulfilling of the law. *(NRSV)*

Suggestions for action

Is there someone close to home who needs your help? Have you received an appeal from a charity recently that you have ignored or forgotten about? Grasp the nettle, and respond.

Closing prayer

Sovereign God,
    teach me to hear your voice in the cry of the poor,
    the hungry, the sick and the oppressed,
    and teach me, in responding to them,
    to respond to you.
Through Jesus Christ my Lord.
Amen.

Sixth week
Love yourself

Opening prayer

O blessed Lord,
    we ask you to pour down upon us such grace
    as may not only cleanse this life of ours,
    but beautify it a little, if it be your will,
    before we go hence and are no more seen.
Grant that we may love you with all our heart,
    and soul,
    and mind,
    and strength,
    and our neighbour as ourselves,
    and that we may persevere unto the end,
    through Jesus Christ our Lord.
Amen.

Rev James Skinner

Introduction

Love yourself! Surely our problem is that we love ourselves over-much already, too full of our own importance, own interests and own ideas. Perhaps so, but are such things the same as loving oneself? On the contrary, selfishness is often not so much a sign of self-love as of self-loathing. A shopping, eating or drinking binge can represent a desperate attempt to disguise a sense of inner emptiness; those who are always talking about themselves may be secretly yearning for acceptance; and those who come across as know-it-alls may be trying to mask a deep-seated insecurity.

    All right, we may say, but can we move from that to talk of loving ourselves? The idea seems at odds with the traditional Christian emphasis on self-sacrifice, humility, service and acknowledging our sinfulness before God. Is that truly the case? It all depends, of course, on what loving self actually means. Naked self-interest has no place in Christian discipleship, but neither has self-denigration. If we move from one to the other, we not only achieve nothing but turn what ought to be a gospel of liberation into one of imprisonment. 'Love your neighbour *as yourself*,' said Jesus, and he meant it. There is not one commandment here, but two, and each is equally important!

Activity

Jumbled words (see page 82).

Reading: Luke 5:4-11

When [Jesus] had finished speaking, he said to Simon, 'Put out into the deep water and let down your nets for a catch.' Simon answered, 'Master, we have worked all night long but have caught nothing. Yet if you say so, I will lay down the nets.' When they had done this, they caught so many fish that their nets were beginning to break. So they signalled to their partners in the other boat to come and help them. And they came and filled both boats, so that they began to sink. But when Simon Peter saw it, he fell down at Jesus' knees, saying, 'Go away from me, Lord, for I am a sinful man!' For he and all who were with him were amazed at the catch of fish that they had taken; and so also were James and John, sons of Zebedee, who were partners with Simon. Then Jesus said to Simon, 'Do not be afraid; from now on you will be catching people.' When they had brought their boats to shore, they left everything and followed him. (*NRSV*)

Comment

It was by no means an unusual story, but it was still shocking: a teenager suffering from anorexia, reduced to little more than a living skeleton, pitiful to behold, yet still convinced she was overweight and hence resolved to diet further. She was one more statistic added to the list of those who have felt they must be sylphlike to be attractive. The whole gamut of eating disorders received considerable media attention when the late Diana, Princess of Wales, spoke publicly of her long battle with bulimia, but such disorders are by no means the only manifestation of the pressures we face in society, concern over our weight or figure just one cause among many of a sense of inadequacy. Probably very few people feel completely happy with who and what they are. Some are conscious of physical features or blemishes that they regard as disfiguring. Others feel socially, academically or physically inferior, while others still are simply self-conscious, lacking in confidence or even painfully shy by dint of their genes, their upbringing or a combination of both. All of us are more than capable of being selfish, self-opinionated and self-indulgent, but that doesn't mean we love ourselves. Far from it – those very characteristics may, deep down, lead to a sense of personal inadequacy, even self-loathing. For all the hi-tech advances and material blessings of our modern world, there is little sign that people are happier today than they once were. All too many continue to wrestle with the debilitating impact of a negative self-image, searching desperately for a sense of identity and worth in an apparently impersonal universe.

So what does faith have to say concerning this? Disturbingly, its contribution has not always been positive, undue emphasis often being placed on human sinfulness and our unworthiness before God. Such teaching contains an important truth, for we are indeed all imperfect, yet the key message at the heart of the gospel is not that we are unworthy but that God, through his grace, loves us for who we are, warts and all. That truth was embodied in the ministry of Jesus, as he repeatedly raised eyebrows through associating with tax collectors, prostitutes and 'sinners', those whom society, including the religious establishment, dismissed as worthless. Where others condemned, he accepted; where they saw the worst, he saw the best. Certainly, there were areas in their lives where he urged change, things that were not as they should be, but love was not conditional upon reform; reform, rather, followed from being loved. If there is one message that radiates from every personal encounter with Jesus recorded in the Scriptures, it is surely this: 'love yourself, value yourself, just as God loves and values you'. The context and nature of such encounters may vary, but the underlying theme remains constant.

Key moments from the stories of two individuals serve to illustrate the point. The first is Simon Peter, as seen in our reading above. Confronted by the power of Jesus, and recognising that he was invested with divine authority, he was immediately overwhelmed by a sense of inadequacy and worthlessness, so that 'he fell down at Jesus' knees, saying, "Go away from me, Lord, for I am a sinful man!"' (Luke 5:8b, *NRSV*). The response is reminiscent of the prophet Isaiah – 'Woe is me! I am lost, for I am a man of unclean lips, and I live among a people of unclean lips; yet my eyes have seen the King, the Lord of hosts!' (Isaiah 6:5, *NRSV*) – he similarly consumed by a sense of sinfulness. On one level, this is a perfectly natural human reaction. To measure oneself against anyone can be a humbling experience; to measure oneself against God brings a contrast that can be hard to bear. Yet if Peter felt he was beyond the pale, Jesus felt very differently. He not only accepted Peter but also wanted him to be a follower, a disciple, and, more than that, a key figure in his purpose, an ambassador for his kingdom and agent in its growth. Sinful he might have been, but that did not diminish his value as a person or the worth that Jesus placed on him. He was a child of God, no more, no less.

The second example is Zacchaeus. Ironically, his story is largely remembered due to his size, his smallness leading him to climb a sycamore tree in order to catch sight of Jesus as he passed by. Perhaps size *was* an issue for him – who knows? Perhaps a resulting sense of grievance at feeling socially excluded led him to take on the despised role of tax collector on behalf of the Roman authorities.

Whatever his reasons, that role must surely have exacerbated a negative self-image, for in the eyes of his fellow citizens it was synonymous with selling out to the enemy. Add to that possible feelings of guilt concerning those he'd swindled during the course of his duties, and we gain some insight into the various factors that must have played on his psyche, undermining his sense of worth. Deep within was an urgent need for acceptance; a fact that *Jesus* recognised even if Zacchaeus struggled to see it himself. 'Zacchaeus,' says Jesus, looking up into the tree, 'hurry and come down; for I must stay at your house today' (Luke 19:5b, *NRSV*). This time there was no protest of unworthiness, simply an eager response and throwing open of his home paralleled by a throwing open of his life. For the first time in years, he was accepted as a person, an individual in his own right. More than that, through rediscovering a sense of worth, he instinctively reached out to others, giving back fourfold to those he had defrauded, and giving to the poor from his plenty. Here is an illustration of that often-noted truth that we can only love our neighbour when we have first learned to love ourselves. From a twisted individual turned in on his own problems and seeking solace in self-interest, Zacchaeus' heart was opened to others through God opening his heart to him in Christ.

Love yourself. We're not talking here about self-interest and self-centredness, looking after number one and never mind the rest. We're not encouraging a cosy complacency, putting our own comforts before the needs of others. We're not justifying conceit, greed or envy. We're talking of an ability to be honest with self, fully recognising our faults and weaknesses and yearning to be better, yet knowing nonetheless that we are valued and loved – that, in God's eyes, we have a right to be here. Far from turning us in on ourselves, such self-acceptance frees us truly to embrace others and life in all its fullness. Too many people struggle through life burdened by a sense of inadequacy. Too often the Church has added to a sense of worthlessness rather than self-esteem. Too frequently the gospel has been presented in terms of negatives rather than positives, of faults rather than forgiveness, and guilt rather than grace. No, God doesn't want any of us to be full of self, thrusting ourselves forward and indifferent to others, but neither does he want us to be cowed, subservient or self-denying. Like Peter and Zacchaeus, and so many others since, he wants us to discover an inner peace, an acceptance of self, an understanding that he values each of us as unique and precious individuals. Don't be fooled: that is not an extra to the gospel, a side issue – it is the gospel itself, writ large. Learn to love yourself, or you will not have learned what it means to love or be loved at all.

Summary

- Few people are altogether happy with who and what they are. Most wrestle with feelings of personal inadequacy, however successfully they may conceal it.

- The Church has sometimes contributed to a negative self-image, faith being presented in terms of negatives rather than positives, and guilt and sin being emphasised at the cost of forgiveness.

- Throughout the Gospels, however, we see Jesus mixing with and welcoming those who society deemed as unacceptable and worthless.

- Peter's response to Christ when he first glimpsed the power of God within him was to stress his own unworthiness. Yet Jesus not only accepted him but also invited him to share in the work of his kingdom.

- Zacchaeus similarly found acceptance through Christ, and, in consequence, was set free to love others. His story illustrates the need to love our neighbour *as ourselves.*

- Love of self is not the same thing as selfishness. On the contrary, it delivers us from the things that hold us captive to self, freeing us to reach out to others.

- In this sense, learning to love self is not incidental to the gospel but at its heart.

Discussion

- Is it true that we tend to be our own sternest critics? Do we dwell sometimes on our bad points at the expense of the good? Why?
- How far should we feel a sense of unworthiness before God? Do you think we can emphasise this too much? Do you feel that negative aspects of the gospel are sometimes stressed instead of the positive?
- What would we describe as the essential ingredients of loving self? What do we find hardest about ourselves to accept?

Prayer

Gracious God,
    we do not find it easy to love ourselves,
    despite the way it may seem.
We find it hard not to dwell on our weaknesses
    rather than focus on our strengths,
    not to brood about mistakes and failures
    rather than rejoice in the things we have achieved.
When we look inside,
    we see the faults and ugliness
    that we try to hide from the world,
    and we find the reality too painful to contemplate,
    so we try to push it away once more.
Yet somehow, despite all that is wrong,
    you have reached out and accepted us as we are,
    with all our faults and weaknesses,
    all our faithlessness and disobedience.
You look deep into our hearts,
    and where we see ugliness, you see someone infinitely precious,
    so valuable that you were willing to endure death on a cross
    to draw us to yourself.
Gracious God,
    we thank you that you love us despite everything,

that you value us not for what we might become
but for what we are.
Teach us to live each day
in the light of that incredible yet wonderful truth
that you love us completely
and want us to be at peace with ourselves and with you.
In Christ's name we ask it.
Amen.

Meditation of the scribe

He made it all sound so easy,
 so simple.
The whole Law,
 everything we'd been struggling to understand
 for so many years,
 summed up in two little commandments:
 you shall love the Lord your God with all your
 heart and mind and soul;
 you shall love your neighbour as yourself.
It sounds perfect, doesn't it?
What our faith is all about, put into a nutshell.
And for the most part I agreed with him –
 spot on!
Love God,
 love your neighbour;
 I've no problem with that –
 it's what I've tried to do all my life.
But love your neighbour as yourself –
 that's where I come unstuck;
 for though you may not believe it,
 and though it may rarely seem like it,
 I don't love myself at all.
Oh, I give a good impression, I know –
 I'm as selfish as the next person,

invariably putting *my* interests before others,
more often than not wrapped up in my own affairs –
I can't deny that.
But beneath the facade,
whenever I have the courage to look deep inside,
I'm ashamed of what I see,
ashamed of what I am.
Love myself?
With all my weakness,
all my greed,
all my pride?
You must be joking!
Only he wasn't, that's the mystery;
there was no irony from Jesus when he said those words,
no sarcasm,
no hidden agenda.
Love your neighbour as yourself, he told us,
and he meant it;
he actually believed that I was lovable.
I just can't tell you what that means,
what hope it gives me –
him to say such a thing, of all people!
For he was under no illusions,
no false sense of my worthiness.
He knew me better than any man,
just as I was,
with all my faults,
all my ugliness,
yet still believed I was worth something.
Am I convinced?
Well, not as much as I'd like to be,
for there are still times when I look at myself
and turn away in shame.
I'm nothing special,
not a nice person at all when you get down to it.
But I've begun to understand that inside this stranger I call me,

beneath the mask I put on for the world,
there's a person whom God truly values,
an individual unique and precious to him,
and if *he* believes that, despite everything, who am *I* to argue?

Further reading: Leviticus 19:18

You shall not seek vengeance or nurse a grievance against any of your people, but you shall love your neighbour as yourself: I am the Lord.

Suggestions for action

Instead of focusing on your faults, thank God for his forgiveness. Instead of dwelling on prayers of confession, offer thanksgiving for his unfailing grace that goes on affirming us each day.

Closing prayer

Gracious God,
   I thank you for loving me before I ever loved you,
   and for continuing to love me
   even when I find it hard to love myself.
Teach me to accept what I am
   and so to grow into what I can become,
   through Jesus Christ my Lord.
Amen.

Appendix 1

Activities

First week: God is love

Hymns of love

The following quiz is concerned with hymns expressing the nature of God as love. (Note: the wording of some hymns may vary slightly from that known to participants in the group.)

1. In which hymn do we find these words?

   > my shepherd is beside me,
   > and nothing can I lack

2. Who wrote the hymn 'Love divine, all loves excelling'?

3. What popular Christmas hymn by Christina Rossetti explores the theme of love?

4. In which hymn do we find these words?

   > . . . he is holding
   > all the world in one embrace.

   and

   > all the sorrow, all the aching,
   > wrings with pain the heart of God.

5. The first four lines in the last verse of John Gowans' popular hymn 'You can't stop rain from falling down' go like this:

   > You can't stop God from loving you,
   >   though you may disobey him;
   > you can't stop God from loving you,
   >   however you betray him:

   Can you supply the closing four lines?

6. Which celebrated hymn was written by George Matheson?

7. Which hymn based on the twenty-third psalm has the word 'love' in the title?

8. In the hymn by Robert Walmsley, 'Come let us sing of a wonderful love', what lines follow this opening line to complete the first verse?

9. Which hymn by Samuel Crossman (1614-83) includes the following lines?

> no story so divine;
> never was love, dear king!
> Never was grief like thine.

10. In what hymn do we find the following chorus?

> Richer than gold is the love of my Lord:
> better than splendour or wealth.

Afterwards, talk briefly together about which hymns speak most powerfully to members of the group.

Second week: Love God

Myths, legends, gods and goddesses quiz

This quiz is about gods and goddesses in myths, legends or modern-day religions. Can you identify them?

1. What was the name of the Babylonian goddess of love and fertility?

2. Which Hindu god is sometimes worshipped as a god of love and fertility?

3. What was the name of the Norse / Viking goddess of love?

4. What was the name of the Egyptian goddess of love?

5. What was the name of the Greek god of love?

6. What was the name of the Roman god of love?

7. What is the name of the Afro-Caribbean goddess of love, beauty and sex?

8. What is the name of the Indian god of love?

9. What was the name of the Roman goddess of love?

10. What was the name of the Greek goddess of love?

Afterwards, talk briefly together about the most appropriate way of expressing our love of God.

Third week: Love one another

Pop music quiz

The following classic pop songs all took love as their theme. Can you remember who sang them?

1. 'You've lost that lovin' feelin''
2. 'Love changes everything'
3. 'The power of love'
4. 'Love is a many splendoured thing'
5. 'I will always love you' (1993 version)
6. 'All you need is love'
7. 'Love is in the air'
8. 'Love me for a reason'
9. 'Love me tender'
10. 'True love ways'

Afterwards, briefly discuss what the word 'love' means and what Jesus meant when he called us to 'love one another'.

Fourth week: Love your enemies

Enemies quiz

1. Which British chieftain had his life spared by the Roman emperor Claudius, even though, as leader of the Catuvellauni tribe, he had fought doggedly against the Romans?

2. Which English king spared the life of his arch-rival for the throne, Matilda, and ultimately recognised her son as his heir?

3. Who said, 'I have decided to stick with love. Hate is too great a burden to bear'?

4. Which film of 1991 starred Julia Roberts in one of the lead roles?

5. Which classic series of children's books featured a friendship between the two foxes Charmer and Ranger, members of the rival red and blue fox families?

6. Which classic novel set in the West Country revolves around a love affair that crosses a bitter family divide?

7. Who memorably declared he felt no ill will towards the perpetrators of the Enniskillen bomb blast in which he was injured and his daughter Marie was killed?

8. Which Indian activist will be forever associated with the principle of non-violence?

9. What unforgettable incident during the First World War occurred on Christmas Day 1914?

Afterwards, talk briefly together about the qualities it takes to love and forgive an enemy.

Fifth week: Love your neighbour

Neighbours quiz

The answers to the following quiz are all different kinds of neighbours.

1. In what year was the Neighbourhood Watch scheme started? Can you describe the scheme's logo?

2. Who might you find living in Ramsay Street?

3. Can you name the neighbouring countries to Brazil?

4. How many people or families in your street can you name?

5. With which location will the names Hilda Ogden, Bet Lynch, Ken Barlow and Mike Baldwin always be associated?

6. Who wrote the hymn, 'When I needed a neighbour, were you there?'

7. Which controversial TV series of the 1970s starred Kath Williams, Jack Smethurst, Nina Baden-Semper and Rudolf Walker, and which parts did they play?

8. In *Eastenders*, which are the neighbouring buildings to the Minute Mart?

9. Name the neighbouring counties to Oxfordshire.

10. In which hymn does the following verse appear? (Note: the wording may vary slightly from that known to participants.)

> Neighbours are both rich and poor,
> neighbours are black, brown and white,
> neighbours are nearby and far away.

Can you remember the next verse to this hymn?

After this quiz, talk together briefly about the opportunities and obstacles to loving our neighbour in our modern world.

Sixth week: Love yourself

Jumbled words

The following jumbled words can all be added to 'self-' to make a compound expression. Can you unravel them?

1. CCOOSSIUN
2. TRENDEC
3. NICENODFT
4. DESTEERTIN
5. FAIRINCCGIS
6. GRIVENS
7. DINEGLUTN
8. INPOONIDATE

9. SDESPOSES

10. GNEIKES

After allowing reasonable time for members of the group to unravel the jumbled words, discuss whether the terms revealed represent qualities or flaws, weaknesses or strengths. Talk briefly together about what loving ourselves should mean, and about the danger of confusing selfishness or egotism with a proper valuing of who and what we are.

Appendix 2

Answers

First week

1. 'In heavenly love abiding'
2. Charles Wesley
3. 'Love came down at Christmas'
4. 'God is love, let heaven adore him'
5. from love like this no power on earth
   the human heart can sever;
   you can't stop God from loving you,
   not God, not now, nor ever.
6. 'O love that will not let me go'
7. 'The King of love my shepherd is'
8. tender and true;
   out of the heart of the Father above,
   streaming to me and to you:
   wonderful love
   dwells in the heart of the Father above.
9. 'My song is love unknown'
10. 'Love is his word, love is his way' by Luke Connaughton

Second week

1. Ishtar
2. Krishna
3. Freya
4. Isis
5. Eros
6. Cupid

7. Oshun
8. Kama
9. Venus
10. Aphrodite

Third week

1. The Righteous Brothers
2. Michael Ball
3. Frankie Goes to Hollywood or Jennifer Rush
4. The Four Aces
5. Whitney Houston
6. The Beatles
7. John Paul Young
8. The Osmonds
9. Elvis Presley
10. Buddy Holly

Fourth week

1. Caractacus
2. Stephen
3. Martin Luther King
4. *Sleeping with the enemy*
5. *The Animals of Farthing Wood*
6. *Lorna Doone*
7. Gordon Wilson
8. Mahatma Gandhi
9. An impromptu football match between German and British forces in 'No man's land'

Fifth week

1. 1982. The logo features a man, woman, child and policeman in a yellow circle, in which is written 'Neighbourhood Watch'
2. Members of the Australian soap opera *Neighbours*
3. Uruguay, Argentina, Paraguay, Bolivia, Peru, Colombia, Venezuela, Guyana, Surinam and French Guiana
4. (Answers will vary)
5. *Coronation Street*
6. Sydney Carter
7. *Love Thy Neighbour*: Joan Booth, Eddie Booth, Barbie Reynolds and Bill Reynolds respectively
8. The Queen Vic and the launderette
9. Gloucestershire, Wiltshire, Berkshire, Buckinghamshire, Northamptonshire, Warwickshire
10. 'Kneels at the feet of his friends' (*Yesu, Yesu*) by Tom Colvin

Sixth week

1. *SELF*-CONSCIOUS
2. *SELF*-CENTRED
3. *SELF*-CONFIDENT
4. *SELF*-INTERESTED
5. *SELF*-SACRIFICING
6. *SELF*-SERVING
7. *SELF*-INDULGENT
8. *SELF*-OPINIONATED
9. *SELF*-POSSESSED
10. *SELF*-SEEKING

Also in this series:
Living with questions – exploring faith and doubt
Paul – the man and the mission
Something to share – Communicating the good news
Prayer – the fundamental questions
Unsung gifts – the Spirit at work in the New Testament
Discipleship – the journey of faith
Women of faith – what they teach us

Also by Nick Fawcett:
No ordinary man (books 1 and 2)
Resources for reflective worship on the person of Jesus

Grappling with God (books 1-4)
Old Testament studies for personal and small-group use

The unfolding story
Resources for reflective worship on the Old Testament

To put it another way
Resources for reflective worship on the Parables

Are you listening?
Honest prayers about life

Prayers for all seasons (books 1 and 2)
A comprehensive resource for public worship

Getting it across
One hundred talks for family worship

Decisions, decisions
A Lent study course

Promises, promises
An Advent study course

Daily prayer
A book of daily devotions

All the above titles are available from your local Christian bookshop
or direct from Kevin Mayhew Ltd, telephone 01449 737978,
fax: 01449 737834, email: sales@kevinmayhewltd.com